Face the Facts

The Arms Trade

Richard Bingley

For information, address the publisher:
Raintree, 100 N. LaSalle, Suite 1200, Chicago, IL 60602

Design by Mayer Media
Printed and bound in China.
07 06 05 04 03
10 9 8 7 6 5 4 3 2 1

Library of Congress Cataloging-in-Publication Data

Bingley, Richard.
  The arms trade / Richard Bingley.
    p. cm. -- (Face the facts)
Summary: Summaries the arguments in the debate over the selling of arms,
from small pistols to military computers, provides facts and figures,
and suggests solutions to the problems associated with this industry.
Includes bibliographical references and index.
  ISBN 0-7398-6431-9 (HC),1-4109-0046-0 (Pbk.)
1. Defense industries. 2. Arms transfers. [1. Defense industries. 2.
Arms transfers. 3. Arms control.] I. Title. II. Series.
  HD9743.A2 B52 2003
  382'.456234--dc21
                          2002013051

Acknowledgments
The publishers would like to thank the following for permission to reproduce photographs:
pp. 4, 16 Digital Vision; pp. 5, 7, 20, 22–23, 44, 46–47 Reuters/Popperfoto; pp. 6, 9, 12, 16 IWM/TRH Pictures; p. 11 Pavel Rahman/Associated Press; pp. 14–15, 30 Peter Newmark's Pictures; p. 13 Associated Press/Topham Picturepoint; p. 14, 17, 19, 35 Topham Picturepoint; pp. 18, 28, 29 Bettman/Corbis; p. 25 Adam Butler/Associated Press; pp. 26, 48–49 TRH Pictures; p. 31 Robert Patrick/Sygma/Corbis; p. 33 David Hartley/Rex Features; pp. 36–37 Defence Picture Library; pp. 38–39 Mark Edwards/Still Pictures; p. 40 Bud Freund/Corbis Digital Stock; p. 41 Brennan Linsley/Associated Press; p. 43 Mark Peters/Rex Features; p. 45 Carlos Guarita/Still Pictures; p. 51 Gary Trotter/Still Pictures.

Cover photograph: Topham Picturepoint

Every effort has been made to contact copyright holders of any material reproduced in this book. Any omissions will be rectified in subsequent printings if notice is given to the publishers.

Some words are shown in bold, **like this.** You can find out what they mean by looking in the Glossary.

Contents

What Is the Arms Trade?
Introduction 4
What Is the Arms Trade? 6
The Legal Arms Trade 8
The Illegal Arms Trade .10
Case Study: Afghanistan 12

History of the Arms Trade
The Origins of the Arms Trade 14
World at War 16
The Cold War 1945–1991 18
Post–Cold War 20

The Effects of the Arms Trade Today
Small Arms 22
Case Study: Conflict Diamonds 24
Conventional Weapons 26
Weapons of Mass Destruction 28
Chemical and Biological Weapons 30
Globalization 32
Popular Culture 34

The Debate About the Arms Trade
Arguments for the Arms Trade 36
Arguments Against the Arms Trade 38
What Is Being Done to Control the Arms Trade? 40
Other International Agreements 42
Governments, NGOs, and Trade Associations . . .44
Getting Involved 46
Facts and Figures 50
Further Information 52
Glossary 54
Index 56

Introduction

The arms trade is an industry like any other. Just as some companies produce food or materials to sell abroad, others sell arms. The arms trade covers the buying and selling of weapons systems, and arms sales are often referred to as defense **exports.** Arms can range from small pistols to high-tech jet aircraft or military computers. Also included in the trade are weapon **components,** such as electronics.

Many industries have both good and bad effects at the same time. Nuclear power, for example, is a way to generate huge amounts of electricity for our homes, but it can also be used to make bombs that could destroy the world. The arms trade creates similar difficulties. Arms have helped countries and individuals defend themselves against aggression, but there are countless occasions where weapons have been used to terrorize defenseless communities.

The F-18 Hornet fighter aircraft, made in the United States by McDonnell Douglas (part of Boeing), has been sold to Australia, Canada, Finland, Kuwait, Malaysia, Spain, and Switzerland. Each plane costs $7 million to make.

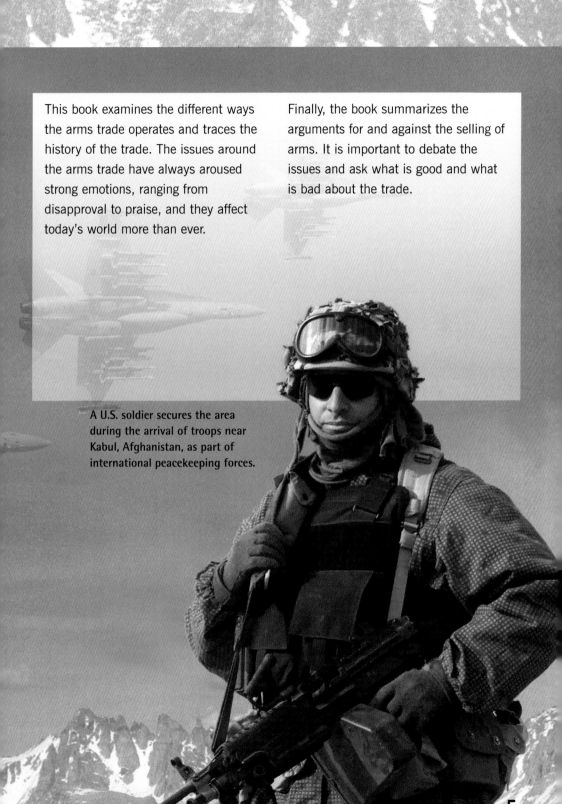

This book examines the different ways the arms trade operates and traces the history of the trade. The issues around the arms trade have always aroused strong emotions, ranging from disapproval to praise, and they affect today's world more than ever.

Finally, the book summarizes the arguments for and against the selling of arms. It is important to debate the issues and ask what is good and what is bad about the trade.

A U.S. soldier secures the area during the arrival of troops near Kabul, Afghanistan, as part of international peacekeeping forces.

What Is the Arms Trade?

Aside from people buying guns for sports such as hunting and target shooting, and citizens who purchase arms for personal and family safety, arms are bought by three groups of people: governments, known as **state actors,** whose countries may not produce adequate equipment to defend themselves or launch military operations; **nonstate actors,** usually groups committed to overthrowing governments; and criminals, who want to seize money, property, or people.

Legal trade

Today most of the arms trade is **legal** and takes place publicly between countries. Each country has a slightly different set of legal rules, but most governments that allow arms to be sold abroad (by granting **export licenses**) say that their arms **exports** should not be used for unprovoked aggression. They should also not be used against the country that sells them.

There are many cases where such rules seem to have been ignored. Many people criticize the legal trade, because arms are sometimes sold to countries with brutal or aggressive regimes. Yet defense exporters point out that they do not know beforehand how arms will be used, and that these cases are exceptional rather than normal.

Illegally traded weapons are often small arms, such as this double-action pistol, that are easy to conceal.

Illegal trade

Just as in other trades, arms dealing is sometimes undertaken illegally. This may be done by people who support a particular cause where a minority is fighting against an armed state, or by people wishing to profit from the situation in troubled areas.

It is difficult to steal a warship or a jet fighter, so illegal arms tend to be small arms such as pistols, rifles, machine guns, and even mortar bombs. These are portable, easy to smuggle and hide, and cheap enough to sell quickly.

An Indonesian customs officer guards these confiscated arms.

The Legal Arms Trade

Arms are sold **legally** from two main sources: government defense departments, and private or state-owned companies.

A government defense department is responsible for the country's armed forces and military equipment. When a defense department buys new equipment or has a **surplus,** it will sometimes sell older weapons abroad. The **reunification** of Germany provides a good example.

After World War II, Germany was split into two separate countries, East and West Germany. In 1990 they were reunified into one country and needed only one army and navy, so the East German naval fleet was sold to Indonesia.

In 2001 Germany's defense department offered secondhand arms, including mortar bombs, fighter planes, tanks, and submarines, to an approved list of 50 countries that had friendly relations with Germany. Private or state-owned companies will usually sell both to their home country's defense department and

abroad. Orders from abroad help keep the production lines running if the home country's needs are not high. The huge profits from such exports are one of many reasons the arms trade is seen differently from other businesses.

This photograph shows the Super Lynx helicopter that was made by GKN–Westland in Britain.

Many jobs depend on winning one large contract; in the following case, senior politicians such as the British and Swedish prime ministers visited South Africa to support bids from their countries. Due to the enormous pressure to win such important contracts, there also tend to be more allegations of **"sweeteners"** in the arms trade than in other business practices. This means that governments and suppliers negotiate arms deals using offers of rewards or even bribes. Over 40 allegations of this kind were reported in the two years following the South Africa deal.

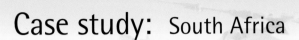

Case study: South Africa

The South African government agreed to spend $4 billion on arms in 1999. Their home defense industry was unable to produce the equipment they needed, so they purchased the following arms.

Equipment	Production company and country
28 fighter jets	BAE Systems-SAAB (Britain and Sweden)
24 fighter trainer jets	BAE Systems-SAAB (Britain and Sweden)
30 light helicopters	Agusta (Italy)
3 submarines	German Submarine Consortium (Germany)
4 Lynx helicopters	GKN-Westland (Britain)

The Illegal Arms Trade

The illegal arms trade is sometimes referred to as an illicit trade, which means it is forbidden. Most illegally or illicitly traded arms tend to be pistols, rifles, machine guns, and even portable antitank and antiaircraft missile systems.

Where do illegal arms come from?

One of the main sources is former war zones. Large amounts of weaponry are circulated during **conflict,** and controls over equipment have usually totally broken down because of the confusion of war. At the end of the conflict, many of these weapons remain hoarded by groups for future use or sale. The 1990s Balkan wars, in the former Republic of Yugoslavia, led to floods of small arms entering European cities.

In some countries gun ownership is more widely permitted than in others, so arms can be bought there and illegally shipped abroad to areas and groups prohibited from receiving **legal** arms sales, perhaps by a **United Nations (UN) embargo,** which is an order to stop the transfer of arms into a country.

Other illegally traded weapons may be stolen from armed forces and police bases around the world. In Australia in 1998, for example, hundreds of assault rifles, grenades, antitank mines, and rocket launchers were stolen from army bases. In communities where guns are more widely allowed, gun shops are raided, too.

Most arms are legally produced and shipped, but may then be **diverted** before reaching their stated destination. In 1999 Polish tanks disappeared after they were officially sold to Yemen. They were reportedly delivered to Sudan, which was under a UN arms embargo at the time.

Many states allow arms exports to other countries, but have weak **export** controls. This is a particular problem in poorer countries that desperately need the money from arms sales.

In certain situations governments secretly support groups or countries by arming them (see Afghanistan case study on page 12). This practice is not always illegal in the supplier country, but often feeds illegal arms sales in the recipient country, since unofficial groups (rebels) often hoard arms to sell or use at a later date.

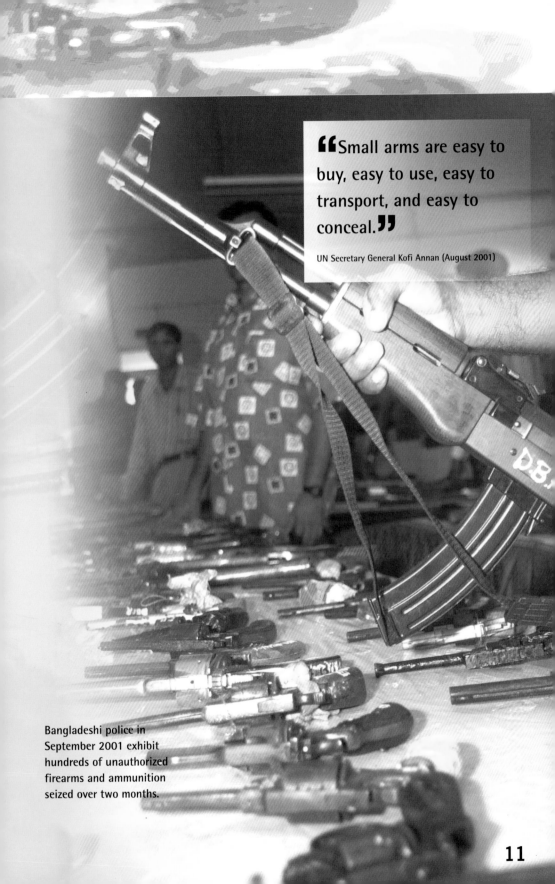

> **"Small arms are easy to buy, easy to use, easy to transport, and easy to conceal."**
>
> UN Secretary General Kofi Annan (August 2001)

Bangladeshi police in September 2001 exhibit hundreds of unauthorized firearms and ammunition seized over two months.

Case Study: Afghanistan

A soldier holds a U.S. Army Stinger.

In 1979 the Soviet Union sent troops into the country to defend the new communist government. When they withdrew ten years later, they had spent $70 billion and lost 14,000 troops. At this time the two **superpowers,** the United States and the Soviet Union, were locked in the **Cold War.** The United States was worried about Soviet actions in Afghanistan, but did not want to risk entering the war. Instead, throughout the 1980s it supplied the Afghan rebels fighting Soviet troops with arms and training. The most famous piece of arms equipment was the Stinger, a shoulder-held missile launcher that terrorized Soviet helicopter pilots

Afghanistan is a strongly Muslim country. In the 1970s the **Soviet Union** was ruled by a **communist** government that wanted to spread communist ideas. Soviet-supported communists seized power in Afghanistan in 1978, inciting revolts by the Afghan people, led by the Mujahideen ("holy warriors").

and is credited with tipping the balance in favor of the Mujahideen.

After the end of Soviet occupation, the United States became concerned that Stingers would be sold abroad and attempted to buy them back. However, by that time many had been hidden by local Afghan groups or sold abroad illegally. This is a good example of how arms can create safety in one instance and danger the next.

Soviet tanks roll through Afghanistan in 1988.

The Origins of the Arms Trade

Arms trading can be traced back to the 14th century with the introduction of gunpowder in Europe. Markets for powder-charged weapons grew as armies demanded cannons and firearms. Arms production as an industry in which weapons were made on a large scale for profit, first developed in Liège, Belgium.

During the industrial revolution in the late 1700s and 1800s, weapons technology advanced quickly. Armies were forced to acquire new equipment when their current weapons became outdated. Many countries had larger armies than ever before. When France attacked Russia in 1812, Napoleon led 500,000 troops—twenty times the size of usual European forces.

Hiram Maxim displays his invention, the first machine gun.

Throughout the 19th century, legendary arms industries emerged. At the age of 14, Alfred Krupp inherited his father's steel company and turned increasingly to making armaments. Half of Krupp's guns were sold outside his native Prussia (now part of Germany) and he established a worldwide reputation as the "Cannon King." In 1866 Austria and Prussia were at war, and Krupp sold guns to both sides. Questions over national loyalty have always hounded arms executives. By the time Krupp died in 1887, he employed 20,000 workers and owned the world's largest arms company.

In Britain, Vickers built warships and sold a new type of gun, the Maxim machine gun. Vickers employed Basil Zaharoff, whose life reads like a movie script. He won orders around the world, which enabled him to marry a Spanish duchess and buy mansions in Paris and Monte Carlo. In the north of England lay the vast factories of Armstrong, which made rifles, ships, and submarines for Italy, Egypt, Turkey, Chile, and the United States. In the United States, the DuPont company supplied gunpowder to Spain and anti-Spanish rebels in Latin America, and armed both Russia and Britain in the Crimean War of 1854.

By the end of the 19th century, the major arms companies had agents around the world mixing with politicians, generals, and royalty. Machine guns and warships now replaced the medieval technology of pistols and cannons. The trade was a leading industry, and had become truly international.

A 77-ton naval gun leaves the Krupp workshops in Essen, 1914.

World at War

Arms traders, who had come to represent modern industrial progress, were at the same time using countries' fears to increase their orders. Arms dealers such as Basil Zaharoff exploited tensions between governments, often of hostile neighboring countries afraid of attack from one another. Once he sold Greece a submarine and frightened its neighbor Turkey into buying two. He then alarmed the Russians with tales of danger from the south, and **Czar** Nicholas II bought four submarines.

Arms production increased during World War I (1914–1918). Profits for the trade soared, with the dramatic demand for equipment. However, the war was disastrous for the image of the industry. In one instance, in the battle of the

Soldiers in trenches prepare for ba during World War I.

Dardanelles, the Germans used British-made guns sold to them by Zaharoff before war broke out, against British troops.

Aircraft, like this Spitfire, became a major part of the arms trade in the 20th century.

The League of Nations was established in 1919 after World War I to promote international cooperation. The League adopted a covenant including six "grave objections" to arms companies, accusing them of playing off one country against another. By the time of World War II (1939–1945), however, the League of Nations was no longer effective as an organization.

Other attempts to control the trade continued. In 1932 an international **disarmament** conference was held in Geneva. In the United States, the Nye Committee investigated effects of the arms trade. This resulted in the formation of the Munitions Control Board, which governed U.S. arms sales, and tried to ensure they did not end up in undesirable places such as war zones. In Britain, Labour Party politicians called for arms factories to be owned by government, reasoning that they could then ensure equipment was not sold to potential enemies.

However, the world changed dramatically during this time. Japanese expansion into China and Hitler's rearmament of German troops with Krupp-made battleships and tanks aroused worldwide concern. World War II provided a spectacular change of fortune for the image of arms manufacturers. British Spitfire fighter planes, made by Vickers Supermarine, and Hawker Hurricanes defeated Germany's Messerschmitt fighter aircraft in the Battle of Britain (1940). A massive aerospace industry grew in the United States, headed by Lockheed Martin and Boeing. This provided the allied forces against Hitler with bombers such as Lockheed's Hudson and Boeing's Flying Fortress. The industry was celebrated by the victors for playing an important part in defending countries against aggression. In the United States, a military super-industry had emerged that was to lead the world arms trade of today and beyond.

The Cold War 1945–199

President John F. Kennedy narrowly avoided a nuclear conflict during the Cuban Missile Crisis in 1962.

For the next 50 years, much of the world split into two opposing camps led by the two **superpowers,** the **Soviet Union** on one side and the United States on the other. Although the two countries resisted direct war, a threatening mood known as the **Cold War** intensified arms production and sales.

The Soviets offered military aid, including arms, to "wars of liberation" involving groups or governments working to overthrow U.S. interests or those of U.S. allies. Similarly, the United States pledged to support any organization fighting **communist** expansion in order to protect their interests abroad. In Latin America the United States sent arms to El Salvador, Honduras, Argentina,

Paraguay, and Venezuela. The Soviet Union countered by sending arms to Cuba, Nicaragua, and Peru.

Most arms deals during this period were an attempt by one superpower to cancel out the power of the other. Arms supplies were principally used as tools to draw countries into or away from **alliances** led by the United States or the Soviet Union. Friendly countries or political groups were rewarded with arms for their support. The United States built alliances because it feared communist ideas might spread and take over on its own soil. The Soviet Union found U.S. worldwide influence threatening, and tried to reduce U.S. power by forming alliances of their own.

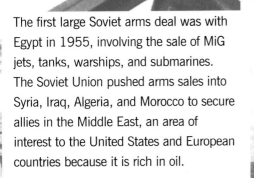

The first large Soviet arms deal was with Egypt in 1955, involving the sale of MiG jets, tanks, warships, and submarines. The Soviet Union pushed arms sales into Syria, Iraq, Algeria, and Morocco to secure allies in the Middle East, an area of interest to the United States and European countries because it is rich in oil.

The arms race

During the Cold War, U.S. and Soviet arms sales reached every continent. By the 1980s the two countries controlled 70 percent of world arms sales. Britain, France, and China made up most of the rest, and $70 billion of arms were sold every year—twice the amount being sold today.

"Every communist must grasp the truth: political power grows out of the barrel of a gun."

Mao Zedong (Chinese leader 1893–1976)

The Berlin Wall was built by the Soviet Union in 1961 to prevent East Germans from escaping to the West. Here seen under construction, it was a striking symbol of the Cold War.

Post-Cold War

Democracy swept through Eastern Europe in the late 1980s, and the **Soviet Union** collapsed in 1991. The Soviet leadership, which had kept its individual states together in opposition to the West, gave way to a more open approach and the beginnings of reform. The major part of the former Soviet Union became known as Russia. With the United States and Russia no longer in open opposition, much of the world felt safer. However, large stocks of weapons remained, many of which would be sold around the world over the years that followed.

Defense exporters had to look for new markets during the 1990s, as arms purchasing programs in Europe, Russia, and the United States shrank due to the new, safer climate. Developing countries of Asia and the Middle East now became the focus of most arms sales, mainly because they contain areas of severe tension. China and Taiwan, the Korean peninsula, Israel and the

United Arab Emirates Air Force staff look over a South African built Skua high speed target drone, during the biggest Middle East arms show, Abu Dhabi, March 1999.

Palestinian territories, and India and Pakistan are all areas where **arms races** often occur. This is because of strong religious, ethnic, or political struggles, which often have a long history. For example, the current conflict between India and Pakistan over Kashmir began as long ago as 1947. India is a mainly Hindu country, although tolerant of other religions, while Pakistan is strongly Muslim. In 1947 the Maharaja (ruler) of Kashmir, fearing internal tribal warfare, opted to join India.

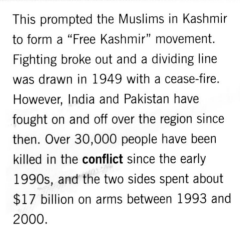

This prompted the Muslims in Kashmir to form a "Free Kashmir" movement. Fighting broke out and a dividing line was drawn in 1949 with a cease-fire. However, India and Pakistan have fought on and off over the region since then. Over 30,000 people have been killed in the **conflict** since the early 1990s, and the two sides spent about $17 billion on arms between 1993 and 2000.

The arms trade remains strong because some parts of the world are still unsafe. Approximately 30 wars were raging every year during the 1990s. Conflicts feed demand for arms. Some argue that the **Cold War** kept many potentially large conflicts from erupting, because the consequences of the United States and the Soviet Union being drawn into direct confrontation would have been catastrophic—perhaps even provoking a a nuclear **holocaust.**

The legal arms trade has almost halved in value since Cold War times, but it is still a huge global business worth over $35 billion annually—almost 1 percent of world trade. With former strict **alliances** gone, countries may sell arms to most state customers without displeasing a **superpower.** A more open arms market has resulted, shaped by economic **globalization.**

Small Arms

Half a million people are killed annually by small arms. Most are **civilians,** not soldiers involved in war. The destructive impact of small arms appears worse than any other sector of the arms trade. The trade is worth around $5 billion per year.

The number of countries producing small arms has grown dramatically. Today they are made **legally** in 95 countries—half the nations on earth. New production adds to the large volume of guns that flooded into many **developing countries** before 1991. The large number of small arms in circulation indicates the difficulty in controlling this part of the arms trade.

The result is that over 500 million guns are in circulation today, or one gun for every 12 people on earth. Firearms are extremely cheap in many areas: in the Sudan, for example, Kalashnikov rifles sell for the price of a chicken.

The availability of small arms in war zones presents a danger, especially for young people. Every year millions experience the death of family members, learning difficulties, eviction from home, and long-term poor health and disability from chaotic conditions in war-torn areas. It is estimated that 4 out of 10 civilian casualties in **conflict** are under 18 years old. Furthermore, there are about 300,000 child soldiers around the world.

They are useful because they are agile, fast, obedient, and cost less to feed. The international community is concerned that more and more children are living in cultures of violence in which the only way to settle a dispute is with a gun, rather than through understanding and dialogue.

Small arms also pose dangers to communities trying to rebuild after war. Immediately after conflict living essentials are often scarce, and structures of law and order may have broken down. Armed gangs or political groups sometimes believe they can get more resources through armed violence than they can by following peaceful channels.

Because small weapons are more widely available, they are more widely used, whether by African cattle rustlers or criminal gangs in cities around the world. Such problems feed a feeling of terror; demand for guns grows as people seek to protect themselves.

Solving problems associated with small arms trading has therefore become an increasing priority for international organizations such as the **UN** (see pages 37–38).

"Small arms have been the basic method of mass killing over the past decade."

Robin Cook (British Foreign Secretary 1997–2001)

These men are part of a local village "defense committee" in Banihal, India, 2001.

Case Study: Conflict Diamonds

Sierra Leone in West Africa has been devastated by civil war between Revolutionary United Front (RUF) rebels and government forces. The country is rich in diamond reserves, and in 1990 RUF forces seized control of diamond mining territories.

The RUF sold diamonds, making money to pay for arms. Hence the term **conflict** diamonds. The RUF is known as one of the world's most brutal rebel groups, commonly amputating victims' limbs and forcing children into combat.

The **UN** introduced arms **embargoes** and asked diamond-trading nations to ensure that conflict diamonds were not sold in their shops. Despite UN requests, arms supplies to RUF forces continued. Planeloads of rifles, machine guns, rocket grenades, and missiles came from the Ukraine into Burkina Faso, a country next to Sierra Leone. The UN reported that arms from other former Soviet and Eastern European countries were flown to Burkina Faso, then transferred to the RUF in Sierra Leone. The Burkina Faso government was paid in diamonds.

RUF diamonds were also traded into Liberia, another neighbor, in exchange for arms and military training. Sierra Leone's government found it difficult to cope with the wealthy RUF. Many government soldiers were disloyal, and the government relied on private security companies to protect diamond and oil reserves. Many of these companies have also been criticized for breaking arms embargoes and buying weapons. Companies caught breaking embargoes can have their directors prosecuted under domestic law. Countries that break embargoes can be placed under diplomatic or economic **sanctions,** although this happens only rarely.

A fourteen-year-old soldier holds a British rifle while patrolling the small town of Ropath in Sierra Leone.

In the late 1990s, the UN sent 8,000 peacekeeping troops to Sierra Leone, but 300 were seized by the RUF. Overall the growth of small arms has lead to the slaughter of thousands of innocent **civilians** in Sierra Leone. But diamond selling, which makes a lot of money for people, stretches beyond the borders of Sierra Leone. The UN reported that "conflict" diamonds had ended up in the large diamond markets of Europe. Worldwide conflict diamond trading is worth $3–7 billion a year. Much of this money is used to buy guns in Africa, helping to make this type of arms trading very difficult to manage.

Conventional Weapons

The **UN** defines larger conventional weapons as battle tanks, combat vehicles, large-caliber artillery systems, combat aircraft, attack helicopters, warships, missiles, and missile launchers.

Conventional equipment costs much more than small arms. A U.S. F-16 fighter jet costs Lockheed Martin around $27 million to make. Conventional arms account for over 80 percent of the world arms trade.

Here are some examples, with their countries of origin:

Tanks:	T-90 (Russia); Challenger 2 (Britain); M1 Abrams (U.S.)
Aircraft:	F-16 (U.S.) speed 1,500 mph (2,400kph); MiG-21 (Russia and China) speed 1,300 mph (2,100kph); Mirage 2000 (France) speed 1,650 mph (2,650kph)
Missiles:	Tomahawk (U.S.) speed 560 mph (900kph); Exocet (France) speed 685 mph (1,100kph)

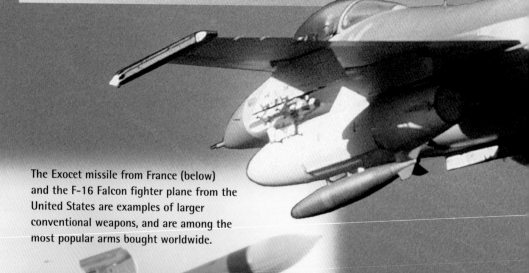

The Exocet missile from France (below) and the F-16 Falcon fighter plane from the United States are examples of larger conventional weapons, and are among the most popular arms bought worldwide.

All these items are for sale. The F-16 is sold extensively around the world, especially in the Middle East. The MiG-21 is used in 47 countries, while the Mirage 2000 is available in 7. Exocet missiles are found in 13 countries including Iraq, while Challenger tanks roam the Middle East.

Although many countries are careful not to sell the latest equipment to states that may attack them, sometimes dealers transfer arms to states where they were not originally intended to go. Recently Saudi Arabia was criticized for selling American missile technology to China.

The UN estimates that 119 of the world's 198 states are involved in conventional arms sales, either as buyers or as sellers. Large arms have now **proliferated** around the world in more areas than ever, so there is less control over the trade than ever before.

Some argue that the world has become more dangerous, since large arms can more easily fall into the wrong hands. However, many arms producers say the spread of larger weapons has deterred large-scale conflict.

"It's important to remember the world is already awash in weapons systems . . . this can have a major impact on planning for peacekeeping operations."

Lt. General James R. Clapper, director of the British Defense Intelligence Agency (1995)

Weapons of Mass Destruction

In 1948 the **UN** introduced a new category of arms called Weapons of Mass Destruction. These include atomic explosives, radioactive material weapons (such as bombs made from uranium or plutonium, which emit radioactivity, causing illness or death from exposure to it), and chemical and biological weapons.

Nuclear weapons

During World War II, the United States, Britain, and the **Soviet Union** feared the German leader Adolph Hitler was developing an atomic bomb. Two German scientists had demonstrated nuclear fission in 1938 by splitting atoms to create powerful explosions. Hitler thought that if he developed an atomic bomb hundreds of times more dangerous than other explosives at the time, important military powers would be too afraid to defend themselves against Germany. In fact, it was the top-secret U.S. Manhattan Project that succeeded in producing the first atomic weapon.

A scarred child survivor from Hiroshima sits in a destroyed schoolroom.

Declared nuclear weapons states:

United States (1945)
Soviet Union, now Russia (1949)
Britain (1952)   France (1960)
China (1964)   India (1998)
Pakistan (1998)

Undeclared:

Israel

(Undeclared means that Israel has nuclear weapons capability but has not publicly declared it.)

Suspected to be developing nuclear weapons:

Iraq   Iran   North Korea

In 1945 allied forces dropped atom bombs on Hiroshima and Nagasaki in Japan. About 67,000 people perished in the first day and a further 36,000 by the end of the year because of injuries and the effects of radiation. This remains the only time atomic bombs have been used in warfare. Most countries treat nuclear weapons with extreme caution now that they know the devastation they can cause.

Since the 1960s international agreements have been made to stop nuclear arms **proliferation.** However, there are reports of scientists moving to nations seeking to develop nuclear weapons, and of materials being moved illegally. This has been a grave concern since Russia's huge nuclear arsenal became poorly guarded and underfunded after the end of the **Cold War.** After the collapse of the Soviet Union, the Russian government was overwhelmed with problems, since the country's industry and economy were severely shaken.

Another problem is that much of the equipment needed to make weapons is also used for peaceful projects, a practice known as **dual-use.** Canada supplied reactors for Pakistan's nuclear energy power stations and the United States did the same for India. Both countries, however, reportedly used the radioactive material in the reactors to develop nuclear weaponry.

Because of strict controls, there is little legal nuclear arms trading. Any sale of this technology tends to be secret and illegal. Nuclear arms sales, therefore, make up a tiny but dangerous fraction of the arms trade.

Hiroshima, Japan, was devastated by the atomic bomb in 1945.

Chemical and Biological Weapons

Some weapons are made from deadly chemicals or bacteria and are designed to poison, choke, or burn people. These are called chemical and biological weapons (CBW), and are almost impossible to trace in the arms trade because they can be made from everyday products such as cleaning fluids.

CBWs are hardly a modern warfare device. The ancient Assyrians and Persians poisoned drinking water, and the Romans used smoke to choke their enemies. In the 1300s an army besieging the Crimean port of Kaffa catapulted plague-infected human bodies over the city walls.

In World War I the French used tear gas and Germany used chlorine, a green-colored gas designed to choke the enemy. Chlorine was readily available as a low-cost industrial product and is more commonly used as a disinfectant agent, especially in swimming pools. Gas masks were soon introduced to reduce the impact of these attacks.

Despite the Geneva Protocol of 1925, which outlawed the use of chemical and biological weapons in war, continuing conflicts and the **Cold War** inspired more dangerous inventions, such as Tabun, mustard gas, and VX gas. Tabun and VX are known as "nerve agents" because they attack the body's nervous system, causing paralysis and breathing difficulties. Mustard gas burns any exposed skin, the lungs, and the eyes. Scandals later erupted in Germany as German companies (innocently, they argued) provided Iraq with chemicals it was able to use against Iran and Kurdish communities in the 1980s.

A machine gun crew on the Somme River during World War I, 1916, wears gas masks.

When **UN** weapons inspectors went into Iraq after the Gulf War (1990–1991) between Iraq and a U.S.-led coalition, they located biological weapons facilities. The use of biological weapons is also known as "germ warfare." Germs such as anthrax were being grown as cultures for possible use as weapons.

At least twenty nations have had chemical and biological weapons programs. Russia reportedly holds the largest CBW stockpile, built up when it was part of the **Soviet Union** (1922–1991). It is very difficult to stop the trade in products such as chlorine or insect spray. This part of the arms trade, more than any other, demonstrates the difficulty of establishing how equipment sold abroad will be used.

> **❝The greatest threat to life on earth is weapons of mass destruction— nuclear, chemical, biological.❞**
>
> Richard Butler (Head of UN Special Commission on Iraq, 1997–1999)

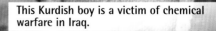

This Kurdish boy is a victim of chemical warfare in Iraq.

Globalization

Globalization occurs when production and sales of goods and services move beyond national boundaries and operate in a "borderless" world. Globalization has increased in the arms trade since the strict **alliances** of the **Cold War** ceased to operate. Free trade (international trade without restrictions) agreements and global communication systems such as the Internet have also contributed.

How is the arms trade becoming global?

National boundaries are becoming increasingly unimportant with the growth of international trade agreements. In Europe and the United States, attempts have been made to introduce free trade agreements for arms trading that will also involve Australia and Japan. Defense **exports** will be shipped to friendly nations without specific permission required for each **component** or project.

To become bigger and more competitive, one company often joins with or purchases another. These mergers are increasingly international. According to **SIPRI** (the Stockholm International Peace Research Institute), 59 arms companies were acquired by European and U.S. defense companies alone between 1998 and 1999.

Companies from different countries also form partnerships, because by sharing technologies, they can make a better end product. This is why arms manufacturers (as well as other large-scale industries) want free trade agreements. For example, manufacturing the Challenger 2 tank in Britain involves 250 smaller companies that all contribute to the product, some of whom are based outside Britain.

Companies sometimes allow foreign companies to make their product under a licensed production agreement. This is an increasingly popular arrangement with those buying arms, because they can assemble the equipment in their own country, generating jobs at home. A recent SIPRI report showed that 14 countries, including Australia, the United States, and Britain, license arms production in 46 other countries.

Globalization in the arms trade has created controversy, because many people claim that controls over weapons sales are becoming fewer when controls are needed more than ever before. Arms manufacturers say that globalization speeds up and improves production and creates a more open and safe world in which countries depend more on each other.

Fact box

Saab (Sweden) and BAE Systems (Britain) are huge aircraft manufacturers in their own rights but recently teamed up to form Gripen International, an alliance that sells fighter jets, and has secured contracts in South Africa and the Czech Republic.

62 KK 23

The Challenger 2 tank is produced in Britain, using 250 international manufacturers to make different parts.

Popular Culture

Films, books, newspapers, and television are important sources of information. The ways in which these media portray subjects such as the arms trade tend to shape our opinions.

Large legal arms sales, like any other business, usually register on financial and foreign pages in more serious newspapers, while arms scandals and illegal activities are given a higher profile. This tends to be the same for television and radio news.

Recently some high-profile campaigns have increased awareness of the arms trade. An international campaign to ban land mines was backed by Britain's Princess Diana. (Her unexpected death in 1997 made headlines the world over.) She visited the former war zones of Angola and Bosnia where many of these explosives lie buried. Followed by media photographers and broadcasters, she was able to show the world amputees who had lost their limbs while going about their normal daily lives, sometimes many years after wars had ended.

In 2002 other arms sales also received international publicity as India and Pakistan almost came to war over the disputed territory of Kashmir. Both sides are armed with nuclear weapons, and had spent billions of dollars on arms supplied from the United States, Britain, China, France, Russia, and Israel. There was great public fear that the consequences of such a huge war would create dangers in other countries.

❝How can countries which manufacture and trade in these weapons square their conscience with such human devastation?❞

Princess Diana (1961–1997), speaking to the Mines Advisory Group and Land Mines Survivors Network, 1997

The James Bond movie *Tomorrow Never Dies* (1997), starring Pierce Brosnan, opens spectacularly on the Russian border at a shadowy snow-covered arms bazaar. Bond destroys the bazaar before taking off in a fighter plane armed with nuclear torpedoes, pursued by MiG jets. This shows a highly glamorized view of the arms trade.

Most arms trade activity occurs in boardrooms, factories, and laboratories and would be of little interest to film directors and authors, but illegal arms trading involving suspicious groups, often with guns, fascinates readers and viewers. The seamy side of the arms trade gets the attention.

Popular culture depicts the arms business as a tiny but dangerous criminal pastime rather than a politically powerful, global industry.

Arguments for the Arms Trade

Although most people individually do not want wars to happen, sadly it is inevitable that they will happen in some form. As long as there are wars, the demand for weapons will support the arms trade.

Suppliers' arguments

The industry, like any other, provides employment, often in highly skilled jobs. About 500,000 people work for the world's 10 largest arms companies. Many communities rely on arms production as the local source of employment. The trade is seen as a useful way for governments to balance their country's finances. Countries always try to reduce the gap between the amount they **import** and the amount they sell abroad.

Making arms for foreign customers keeps production lines running when orders from home are scarce, and enables technological progress to continue. Such progress will benefit armed services at home, because they will get improved weapons systems.

In the right hands, arms can be used positively to keep order and to act as a deterrent against crime.

> **ff Weapons are not the problem, it is the men behind them. 𝕁𝕁**
>
> Gerald Bull (Canadian Artillery and Rocket Manufacturer, 1928–1990)

Warrior armed personnel carriers, produced in Britain by GKN, wait outside the factory to be loaded aboard ships for transport.

If one country refused to sell arms, another country would sell them instead.

Research into arms technology is often responsible for pioneering scientific knowledge and spreading the benefits into other sectors such as agriculture, computing, and communications. The Internet, for example, was first developed for military purposes.

Arms sales can be used to control nations, because nations become reliant on their supplier country. This is helpful when the supplier country wants to build **alliances** or restrain aggressive behavior. Arms traders also gather information about other nations' military strengths.

Consumers' arguments

Countries have the right to protect themselves. Many countries do not make their own arms or have the technology to make high-tech arms that neighboring countries may have.

Countries have a right to decide what products they buy, whether these are weapons or bananas. It is wrong for other countries to tell another what to do with its money.

Arguments Against the Arms Trade

Arms are sometimes deliberately sold into areas of **conflict** and tension. The better-armed countries or **nonstate actors** become, the easier it is for them to be drawn away from peaceful solutions toward the use of weapons. In this way the arms trade does not increase our security but reduces it.

Arms have often been used against soldiers from the countries that sold them in the first place. In the Gulf War, French troops faced attack from Iraqi air forces with Mirage jets, made in France. The United States has been particularly affected by such **boomerang** scenarios. According to an important research group, the Federation of American Scientists, "Past arms **exports** to governments and nonstate actors in Panama, Haiti, Somalia, Iraq, Iran, and especially Afghanistan have all turned into U.S. security threats."

Arms companies are more heavily supported by government than most other industries. According to the Federation of American Scientists, U.S. government support is $6 billion annually, a third of the value of its total sales. Other leading arms exporters, such as Britain, France, and Russia, **subsidize** their arms export industry, too. Some believe this money could be spent on more important items.

❝Every gun that is made, every warship launched, every rocket fired represents, in the final analysis, a theft from those who hunger and are not fed, who are cold and are not clothed.❞

Dwight D. Eisenhower (U.S. President, 1953–1961)

Arms companies promote sales to poorer countries that could be spending their money on water, sanitation, education, and health programs instead of arms. The **UN** classifies 46 countries as Least Developed Countries. Thirty of these are in Africa, where half the population— some 340 million people—lives on less than one U.S. dollar a day.

Many governments that are arms buyers have alarming human rights records, and sometimes arms are used to violate human rights. In Iraq, U.S. helicopters sold for crop spraying were used to attack Kurdish communities with chemical weapons. Continuing to sell arms to governments that misuse them means their behavior is being tolerated.

Children at school in Burkina Faso, where education, along with other services, suffers as in most developing countries. These countries cannot afford arms but often buy them.

What Is Being Done to Control the Arms Trade?

The United Nations

The **UN** was established after World War II "to maintain international peace and security" by developing "friendly relations among nations." Through its Department for Disarmament, it takes action against the worst aspects of the trade. The department previously concentrated more on chemical, biological, and nuclear arms, but it argues that increasing dangers come from small and conventional arms, which have become more widely distributed.

This building in New York holds t UN Headquarters

The UN at work

The UN held its first full-scale conference on the issue of small arms in 2001. Measures to remove guns from war zones when fighting is over were introduced. Wide-ranging proposals about prohibiting private ownership of guns were unsuccessful. The conference agreed to meet again by 2006.

The UN sometimes imposes arms **embargoes,** which means it bans the sale of arms both into and out of **conflict** zones. UN embargoes carry the **authority** of the international community, but the organization does not have the resources to police the arrangements; it relies on states to resist arms sales into those areas. There are countless examples of embargoes being broken. Throughout the 1990s UN embargoes were placed on Angola, Liberia, Sierra Leone, Ethiopia, Eritrea, Yugoslavia, and Afghanistan. However, private arms dealers, sometimes secretly assisted by governments who were eager to make money from old stocks, broke the rules and transported arms into these areas.

This UN peacekeeping soldier is posted in Cambodia.

The UN Register of Conventional Arms was established after worldwide concern arose about huge arms purchases by unstable countries, notably Iraq with its dictatorial rule. The UN invited countries to declare how many weapons they buy and sell. It now estimates that 90 percent of global conventional arms sales are covered in the register. The UN believes too many arms "pose a threat to national, regional, and international peace and security." If states were more open about the quantity of arms they own, they might appear less threatening, and others would then buy fewer arms.

Many people believe the UN's role is important. This is partly because the UN, by calling for **disarmament** measures, officially confirms that elements of the arms trade have caused international hazards. Supporters hope that this will put moral pressure on individual governments to stop weapons from leaving their own country. The most powerful part of the UN is the Security Council. Its five permanent members (United States, Britain, France, Russia, and China) produce up to 85 percent of weapons bought in the world's arms trade. If arms sales are to be better controlled, the organization most likely to achieve the cooperation needed is the UN.

41

Other International Agreements

Various networks of international agreements have been set up to govern the arms trade. Some examples of these arms control measures are given here.

Small arms

The Economic Community of West African States (ECOWAS) made a three-year agreement in 1998 not to buy, sell, or make any small arms. ECOWAS countries include Liberia and Sierra Leone, two nations ravaged by civil war throughout the last decade. According to the **UN**, 2 million lives were lost during the 1980s due to **conflicts** and rebellions, and 7 million small arms were available in the region. This was the first agreement of its kind in the world. However, observers have challenged the effectiveness of the agreement, saying that hardly any Africans knew it existed. Ongoing conflicts in the region have driven the high demand for weapons.

Conventional arms

The Ottawa Convention (1997) banned production, sale, and use of antipersonnel land mines, explosives that are placed in the ground to destroy people. By the start of 2002, it had 142 signatories, although the United States, China, and Russia—the largest producers and exporters of mines—have so far refused to sign. According to the U.S. Department of State, there are approximately 70 million antipersonnel mines buried in the ground of 70 countries, and 250 million more in military stockpiles around the world. More positively, according to the British charity Land Mine Action, 29 countries have reported they have destroyed their stocks.

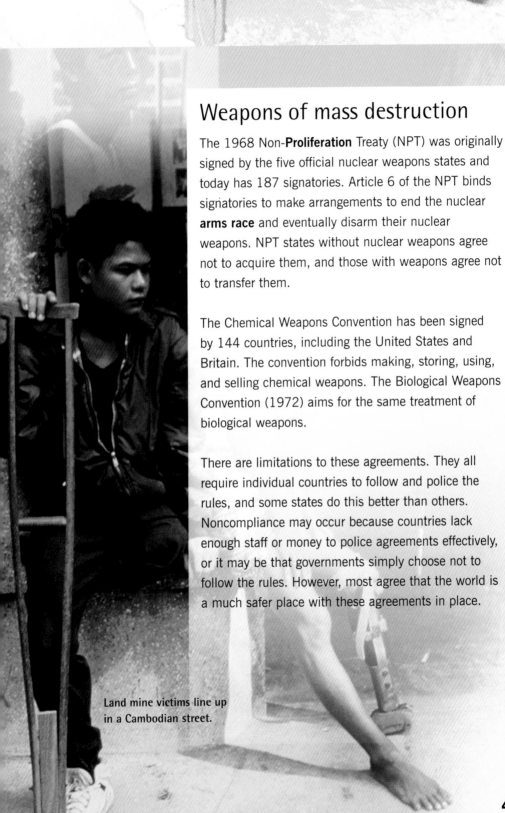

Weapons of mass destruction

The 1968 Non-**Proliferation** Treaty (NPT) was originally signed by the five official nuclear weapons states and today has 187 signatories. Article 6 of the NPT binds signatories to make arrangements to end the nuclear **arms race** and eventually disarm their nuclear weapons. NPT states without nuclear weapons agree not to acquire them, and those with weapons agree not to transfer them.

The Chemical Weapons Convention has been signed by 144 countries, including the United States and Britain. The convention forbids making, storing, using, and selling chemical weapons. The Biological Weapons Convention (1972) aims for the same treatment of biological weapons.

There are limitations to these agreements. They all require individual countries to follow and police the rules, and some states do this better than others. Noncompliance may occur because countries lack enough staff or money to police agreements effectively, or it may be that governments simply choose not to follow the rules. However, most agree that the world is a much safer place with these agreements in place.

Land mine victims line up in a Cambodian street.

Governments, NGOs, and Trade Associations

Each country has its own set of laws controlling defense **exports,** which are made by national governments. However, some states may be less inclined to control where their arms sales end up than others. Because it is important to stop arms from falling into the wrong hands, the **UN** is anxious to introduce a basic standard of behavior. There are many groups of people with different views seeking to influence politicians and decision-makers at national and international levels.

Nongovernmental Organizations (NGOs) are independent of government. They have specialist knowledge of areas of social concern such as civil rights or arms trading. Some NGOs are extremely well known; for example, the human rights organization, Amnesty International, claims to have about a million members and supporters in 162 countries. NGOs seek to change official behavior through research and

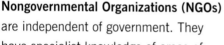

Sabine Christiansen
UNICEF-Botschafterin

Sir Peter Ustinov
UNICEF-Botschafter

A press conference for a UN Children's Emergency Fund (UNICEF) campaign to stop the production and trade of small arms.

publications, advising politicians or celebrity spokespersons, informing the media, recruiting new supporters, campaigns, and public demonstrations. Large NGOs have good access to the media, national lawmaking bodies, and international conferences. At the recent UN Conference on Small Arms, an entire day was allocated to speakers from NGOs around the world, including the International Action Network on Small Arms (IANSA), Oxfam, Amnesty International with Human Rights Watch, and more regional groups such as the Christian Council of Sierra Leone.

Delegates at an armed forces arms fair, where defense industries can display their latest products.

Workers and executives in the arms trade promote their concerns and interests, too. In the United States, the National Defense Industrial Association represents the interests of U.S. workers from 950 companies producing military products. Britain's Defense Manufacturers Association represents the interests of 400,000 defense workers, about 20 percent of whom produce arms exports, while the bulk of the work is on projects for the country's Ministry of Defense. Such organizations advise lawmakers and governments, provide briefings, give media interviews, enlist celebrities, and sponsor defense exhibitions, research, and publications.

The recommendations of defense associations are often (though not always) the opposite of those made by the NGOs. NGOs usually seek to introduce measures to reduce the arms trade, and therefore arms production, while trade associations seek to protect the jobs of their members.

Getting Involved

The arms trade is a deeply controversial global practice. For some it enables states and groups to defend themselves when otherwise they could not. For others it feeds **conflict** and upholds the power of governments that rule their peoples with fear and force. At times it is part of an industry that pioneers technology. At others times **developing countries** may purchase arms with funds that are badly needed for food, healthcare, and education.

What is clear is that the trade affects every one of us. More nations today have strong military capabilities that may one day endanger or save us. We may have relatives or friends who work in defense manufacturing plants that sell some of their products abroad. We may come across one of the 550 million guns in circulation in cities around the world, or when visiting other countries as travelers, workers, or peacekeepers. Many people live in war zones, and many more are refugees from areas where the availability of arms made it impossible to continue living there.

A good way to understand the complicated questions that the arms trade poses for different groups in society is to imagine the points of view of various people involved in the trade. In the event of a conflict between two countries, for example, what would an arms producer, an arms exporter, and someone who lived in a danger zone be thinking? Group role-play can be a good way of exploring the arguments: Should arms sales continue as they do now, or what changes could be made?

A defense expert talks to young visitors at an international defense exhibition.

47

Fighter jets return from liberating
Kuwait after the Gulf War in 1991.

There are many ways to understand more and make your views known about arms trade issues. Sources of further information and contacts are given at the end of this book. The arms trade is constantly changing, so you should try to keep up with developments.

Other good sources of information are the Internet, newsmagazines, and the bigger newspapers, although you should be aware that not all information available (especially on the Internet) is reliable. The foreign and financial pages of newspapers will inform you of large international arms deals and areas of world tension.

Nongovernmental organizations (NGOs) are often good sources of reports and information, although they are usually working against aspects of the arms trade, and their views could be **biased.** They are always looking for support and assistance. Their websites discuss the various campaigns and issues they are currently working on.

Defense manufacturers also give information about their activities on their websites. Most of these companies also produce non-military equipment.

Another way to be actively involved is to write to your local representatives about a topical arms trade issue. Elected officials are happy to hear the views of young people. You should receive an official letter back from them explaining their ideas and policies. Company representatives, local politicians, and people who work for NGOs will often visit schools to talk about their work.

The best way to see past and present military equipment safely is to visit the many military museums and air shows open to the public.

Facts and Figures

Top ten arms buyers in the developing world (1993–2000)

Rank	Country	$ billions –imports	Region
1	Saudi Arabia	24.5	Middle East
2	United Arab Emirates	19.0	Middle East
3	China	12.6	Asia
4	Egypt	11.6	Middle East
5	India	11.5	Asia
6	Israel	9.5	Middle East
7	South Korea	8.1	Asia
8	Kuwait	6.0	Middle East
9	Pakistan	5.3	Asia
10	South Africa	4.7	Africa

Top ten arms companies globally

Rank	Company	Home	$ billions –arms sales
1	Lockheed Martin	United States	18.0
2	Boeing	United States	17.0
3	Raytheon	United States	14.0
4	BAE Systems	United States	13.2
5	General Dynamics	United States	6.5
6	Northrop Grumman	United States	5.6
7	EADS	France	4.6
8	Thales	France	4.3
9	United Technologies	United States	4.1
10	TRW	United States	4.0

A young Cambodian girl carrying an assault rifle prepares to ride her bicycle.

Top conventional arms sellers 1995–1999

Rank	Country	$ billions	Main customers
1	United States	54.4	Taiwan, Saudi Arabia, Egypt, Japan
2	Russia	14.6	China, India
3	France	11.7	Taiwan, UAE
4	Britain	7.3	Saudi Arabia
5	Germany	6.1	Turkey, Greece
6	Netherlands	2.2	UAE, India, Greece
7	China	2.2	Malaysia, Myanmar

Top small arms sellers

Rank	Country	$ millions
1	United States	Over 1,200
2	Germany	384
3	Russia	100–50 (estimated)
4	Brazil	100–150 (estimated)
5	Austria	60
6	Czech Rep.	59
7	Britain	44
8	South Korea	43
9	Sweden	40
10	Poland	40

Further Information

Contacts

Amnesty International
322 8th Avenue
New York, NY 10001
e-mail: admin-us@aiusa.org
www.amnesty.org

Federation of American Scientists
Arms Sales Monitoring Project
1717 K Street NW
Suite 209
Washington, D.C. 20036
(202) 548-3300
e-mail: fas@fas.org
www.fas.org/asmp

Landmine Action
1st floor
89 Albert Embankment
London England SE1 7TP
e-mail: info@landmineaction.org
www.landmineaction.org

National Rifle Association
11250 Waples Mill Road
Fairfax, VA 22030
(800) 231-0752
www.nrahq.org

SIPRI (Stockholm International Peace
Research Institute)
www.sipri.se

United Nations Youth Unit
2 UN Plaza, 13th Floor
New York, NY 10017
e-mail: ilenko@un.org
www.un.org/youth

United Nations
UN Headquarters
First Avenue at 46th Street
New York, NY 10017
www.un.org

Further reading

BOOKS

Gold, Susan Dudley. *Arms Control.*
Brookfield, Conn.: Twenty-First Century
Books, 1997.

McCuen, Gary E., ed. *Biological
Terrorism and Weapons of Mass
Destruction.* Hudson, Wisc.:
GEM/McCuen, 1999.

Meltzer, Milton. *The Day the Sky Fell.*
New York: Random House, 2002.

Torr, James D. *Americans' Views About
War.* Farmington Hills, Mich.: Gale
Group, 2001.

Glossary

alliance   group of countries acting together

arms race   where one state buys arms and other states feel threatened and do the same

authority   person or organization's power to carry out certain actions

bazaar   market

bias   one-sided perspective on an issue

boomerang   aboriginal tool that can return to the place it was thrown from; term used to describe an action that has unwelcome repercussions

civilian   not a member of any armed forces

Cold War   hostile relationship between America and the **Soviet Union**, so called because it never "heated up" into direct war

communist   person who believes the state should control production and distribution

components   parts that make up a final product

conflict   disagreement or war

Czar   emperor of Russia (before 1917)

developing countries   countries that do not have highly developed industry and whose citizens are often poor

disarmament   reduction and abolition of weapons

diverted   when something is redirected away from its intended route

dual-use   products for either military or civilian use

embargo   when countries, regions, or the UN make an order to stop the transfer of arms into or away from an area

export license   certificate from government granting permission to send equipment abroad

exports   goods sold abroad

globalization   where production and sales move beyond national boundaries and operate within a borderless world

holocaust   large-scale destruction

import   buy from abroad

legal   permitted by governments and international law

nongovernmental organizations (NGOs)   independent organizations that try to influence government officials and public opinion on various issues

nonstate actor   rebel group

proliferate   increase or multiply rapidly

proliferation   increase in production and distribution of weapons

reunification reunite separate territories. For example, the joining together of East and West Germany in 1990.

sanctions penalties for disobeying rules

signatory person or government that signs an agreement with other persons or governments

SIPRI (Stockholm International Peace Research Institute) organization that researches and publishes reports on the global arms trade and international peace and security

Soviet Union from 1922 to 1991, a block of fifteen republics controlled by its largest member, Russia

state actor government

subsidize when an organization, such as a government, pays for part or all of a project

superpower nation much more powerful than other nations. The United States and the Soviet Union were the superpowers during the Cold War.

surplus amount left over after requirements are met

"sweetener" favor or bribe given for particular decision

United Nations (UN) international organization of countries set up in 1945 to promote peace, security, and international cooperation. The UN sometimes sends peacekeeping forces to areas in conflict.

Index

Afghanistan 5, 12, 13, 38, 40
Annan, Kofi 11

Berlin Wall 19
biological weapons 28, 30, 31, 40, 43
Bull, Gerald 36
Butler, Richard 31

chemical weapons 28, 30, 31, 39, 40, 43
China 17, 20, 41, 50, 51
  conventional weapons 27
  land mines 42
  nuclear weapons 28
Clapper, James R. 27
Cold War 12, 18, 19, 21, 54
  CBW 30
  globalization 32
  nuclear weapons 29
conventional weapons 26, 27, 40, 42
Cook, Robin 23

Diana, Princess 34

Eisenhower, Dwight D. 38

fighter aircraft 4, 26, 27, 34, 48
  Gulf War 38
  legal trade 8
  World War II 17

Germany 8, 15, 17, 28, 51
globalization 21, 32, 33, 54
Great Britain 41, 51
  arms control 17, 43

arms industry 15, 33, 45
  Crimean War 15
  globalization 32
  nuclear weapons 28
Gulf War 31, 38, 48
helicopters 8, 26, 39
Hitler, Adolph 17, 28

India 23, 28, 29, 50
  Kashmir conflict 21, 34
Iraq 19, 28, 30, 31, 41
  Gulf War 38
  human rights 39

Kennedy, John F. 18
Krupp, Alfred 15, 17

land mines 34, 42, 43

Mao Zedong 19
Maxim, Hiram 14

Napoleon 14
Nicholas II, Czar 16
nuclear weapons 28, 29, 31, 34, 40, 43

Pakistan 21, 28, 29, 34
peacekeeping 5, 27, 46

rifles 22, 51
  arms industry 15
  illegal trade 7, 10
  RUF 24
Russia 51
  arms sales 20
  CBW 31
  Crimean War 15
  land mines 42
  Napoleon 14
  nuclear weapons 29

UN 41
Zaharoff 16

ships 15, 17, 19, 26
Sierra Leone 24, 25
small arms 11, 22, 23
  control 40, 42
  trade 6, 7, 10
  RUF 25
Soviet Union 20, 55
  Afghanistan 12, 13
  CBW 31
  Cold War 18, 19, 21
  nuclear weapons 28, 29
submarines 8, 15, 16, 19

tanks 10, 26, 27, 36
  Cold War 19
  globalization 32, 33
  Second World War 17

UN 40, 41, 52, 55
  conventional weapons 26, 27
  embargoes 10, 24, 40
  Gulf War 31
  small arms 23
United States 32, 38, 41, 51
  Afghanistan 12, 13
  arms industry 15, 20, 43, 45
  Cold War 18, 19, 21
  land mines 42
  nuclear weapons 28

World War I 16, 17, 30
War War II 17

Zaharoff, Basil 15, 16